SCHULTZ

SCALES and CHORDS in all the MAJOR and MINOR KEYS FOR THE PIANO

Revised and Edited by
Willard A. Palmer

AN ALFRED MASTERWORK EDITION

Second Edition

Cover art: Golden Autumn, *1895*
by Isaac Levitan (1860–1900)
Tretyakov Gallery, Moscow, Russia
Scala/Art Resource, New York

About This Book

This popular and practical approach to scale practice, written by F.A.Schulz in the latter part of the 19th century, has remained one of the most useful piano books on the subject of scales, for the following reasons:

1. The order of presentation of the material is most logical. The major scales, together with their relative melodic and harmonic minor scales, are presented in clockwise motion around the circle of 5ths, for sharp and flat keys alike.

2. The scales covered are those most frequently required as routine performance for admission to conservatories, universities and colleges. They include all the scales usually demanded at jury examinations for students aspiring to degrees in music, and they satisfy the requirements for all types of contests, adjudications, ratings, etc., as demanded by various musical associations.

3. Each scale is followed by a cadential chord progression in the following order:

TONIC (I), SUBDOMINANT (IV), TONIC (I), DOMINANT (V), DOMINANT 7th (V^7), TONIC (I).

EXAMPLE (C major):

4. A scale combining the ascending major and the descending melodic minor (pages 14 & 15) gives a strong concept of the similarities and differences in the parallel major and minor scales. This is an important supplement to the presentation of the relative major and minor scales given in the previous pages, and is especially valuable in emphasizing the differences in the fingerings of major and minor scales when they begin on black keys.

This revised edition contains the following improvements, made by the present editor:

1. The major-melodic minor scale combination mentioned in No. 4, above, has been presented in all keys. Since it would be difficult for students to work out the correct fingerings, this makes this feature more practical and useful.

2. A clear explanation of the formation of scales by tetrachords has been added in the opening pages of this edition, together with instructions on the use of the CIRCLE OF 5THS as an aid in learning the order of scales, the relative minors, the key signatures, etc.

3. The one-page presentation of ornaments given in the original edition could only be correctly applied to a limited area of music, namely to some compositions of the late 19th century. This, along with the one-page study of "Triplets Against Even Notes," has been omitted to make room for the additional material offered, which is more relevant to the study of scales.

The Construction Of Scales

A TETRACHORD is a series of four notes in alphabetical order, having a pattern of WHOLE STEP, WHOLE STEP, HALF STEP.

TETRACHORD BEGINNING ON C: **TETRACHORD BEGINNING ON G:** **TETRACHORD BEGINNING ON D:**

A MAJOR SCALE is made of TWO TETRACHORDS joined at a distance of a WHOLE STEP:

C MAJOR SCALE:

The MAJOR SCALE beginning on C is called the C MAJOR SCALE. The RELATED MINOR SCALE beginning on the 6th tone (A) is an A MINOR SCALE. It is commonly referred to as THE RELATIVE MINOR.

The NATURAL or PURE MINOR may be made by playing the notes of the MAJOR SCALE, beginning on the 6th note of the major scale.

A MINOR SCALE (NATURAL OR PURE)

A MELODIC (or diatonic) MINOR SCALE raises the 6th and 7th tones ascending, but descends like the PURE or NATURAL MINOR.

A MINOR SCALE (MELODIC OR DIATONIC)

A HARMONIC MINOR SCALE raises only the 7th tone ascending and descending.

A MINOR SCALE (HARMONIC)

The natural minor scale is found in music based on modes. This book deals only with the more frequently used MAJOR, MELODIC MINOR and HARMONIC MINOR scales.

The Circle Of Fifths

Showing The Relative Major & Minor Keys And Their Signatures

The scales in this book are presented in the order of the keys in the "Circle of 5ths," moving clockwise, beginning with C major and its relative, A minor, each of which have the key signature of no sharps, no flats.

In the following diagram, each major key name on the outside circle is exactly opposite its relative minor key name on the inside circle.

Since the following keys on the piano have two names, scales built on these keys also may have two names:

B	&	Cb	F♯	&	Gb
C♯	&	Db	G♯	&	Ab
D♯	&	Eb	A♯	&	Bb

Such keys and scales are called "enharmonic".

Moving clockwise around the circle, each major and its relative minor gains one sharp with each new segment of the circle. After becoming enharmonic scales with flat key signatures, the scales lose one flat with each clockwise advance around the circle.

The signatures of all the scales are more easily learned by memorizing the order of the sharps (moving clockwise around the circle) and the order of flats (moving counter-clockwise).

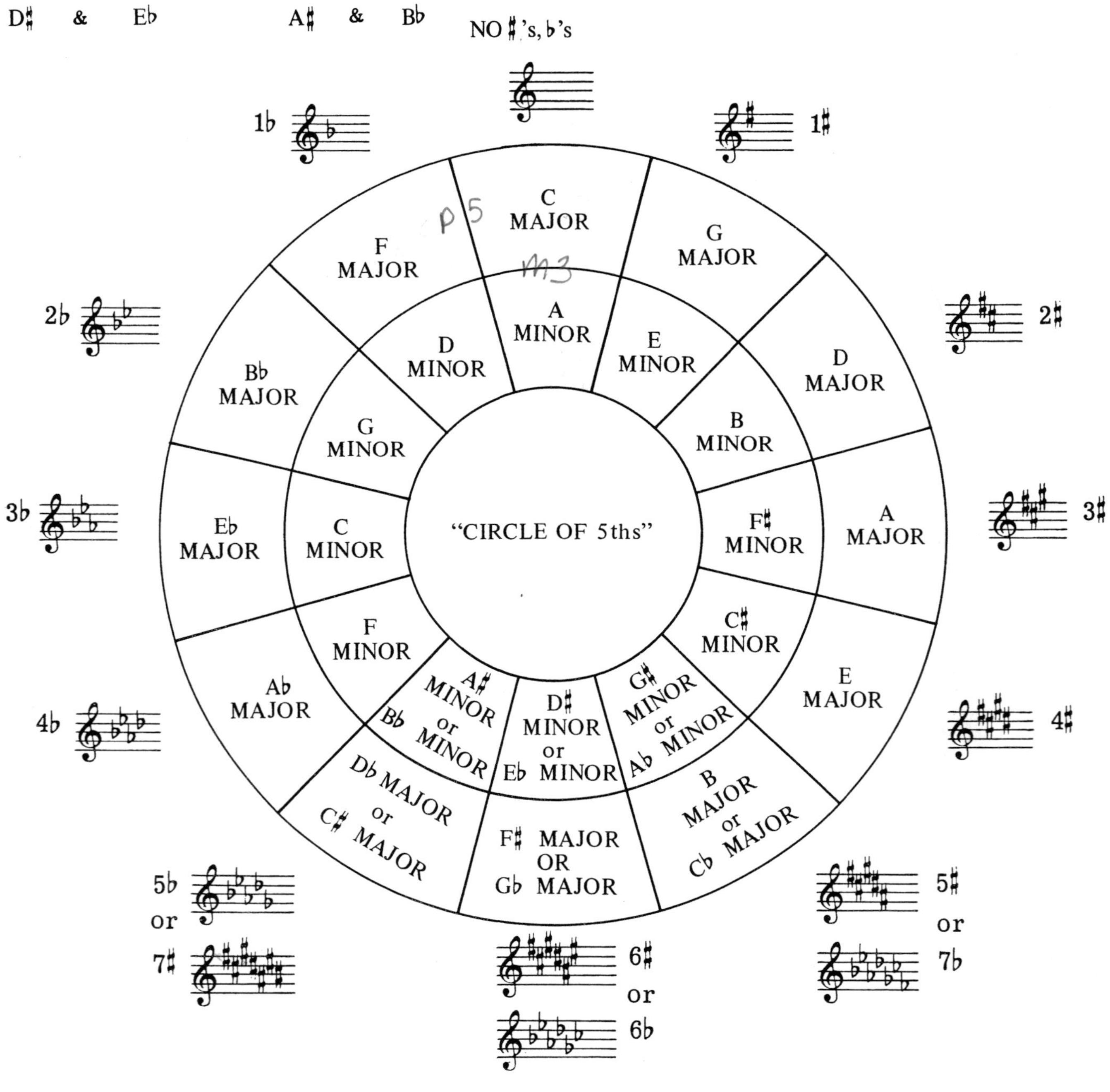

ORDER OF SHARPS IN THE KEY SIGNATURES: F♯, C♯, G♯, D♯, A♯, E♯, B♯.
ORDER OF FLATS IN THE KEY SIGNATURES: Bb, Eb, Ab, Db, Gb, Cb, Fb.

C MAJOR & A MINOR

C major

A minor (melodic)

A minor (harmonic)

G MAJOR & E MINOR

G major

E minor (melodic)

E minor (harmonic)

D MAJOR & B MINOR

D major

B minor (melodic)

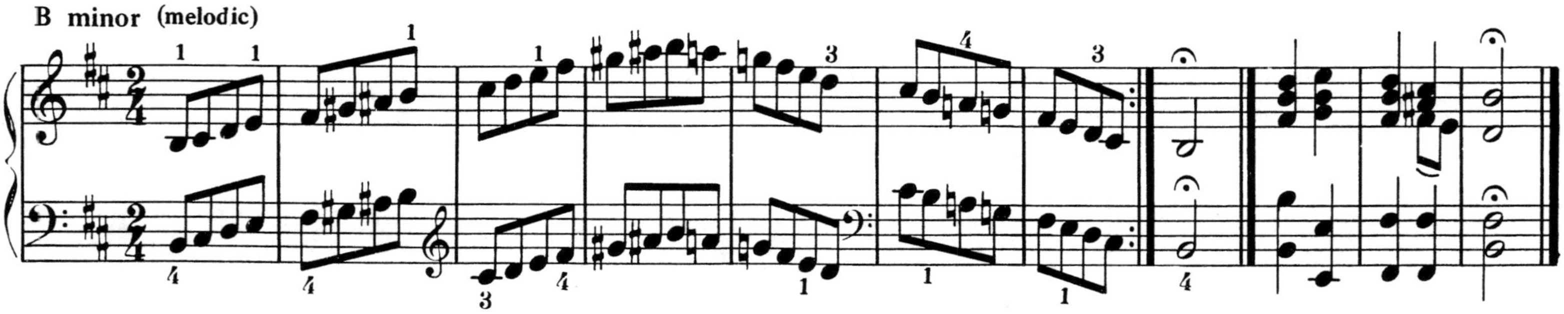

B minor (harmonic)

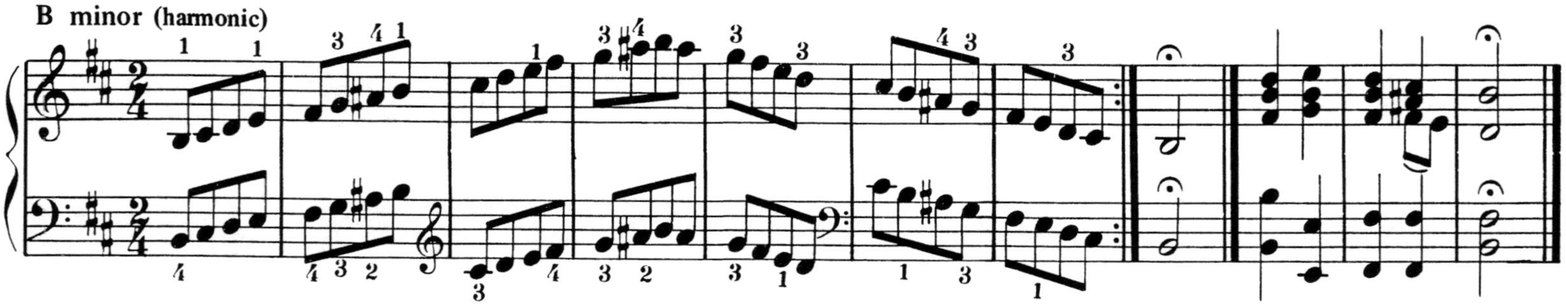

A MAJOR & F♯ MINOR

A major

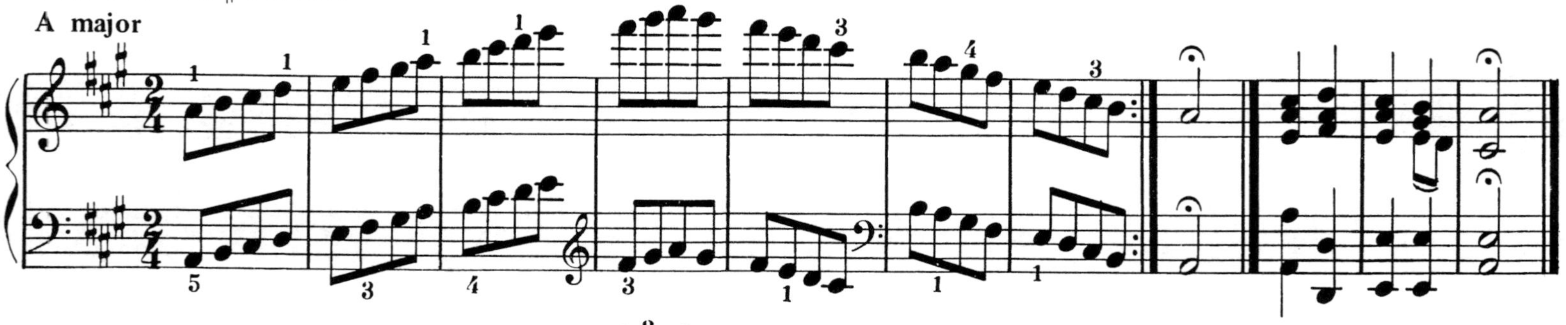

F sharp minor (melodic)

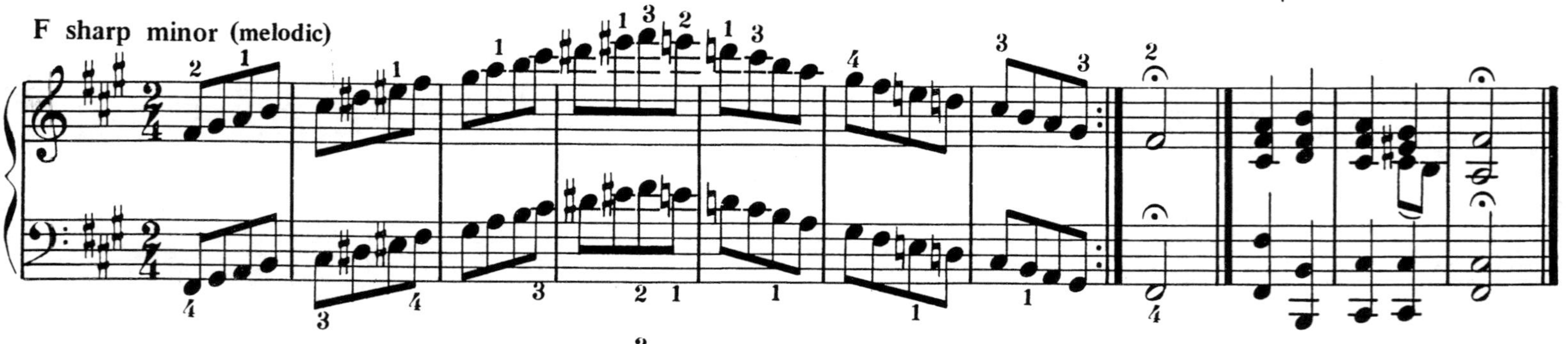

F sharp minor (harmonic)

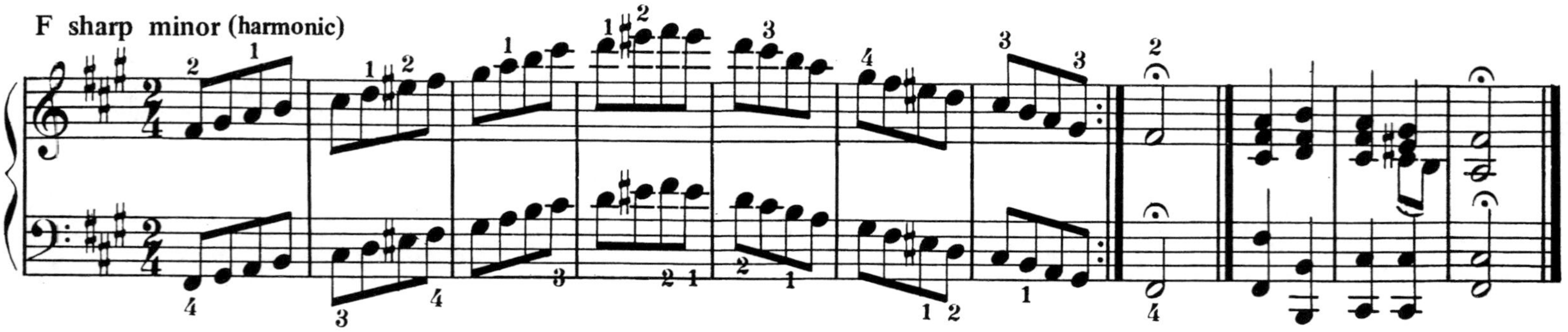

E MAJOR & C♯ MINOR

E major

C sharp minor (melodic)

C sharp minor (harmonic)

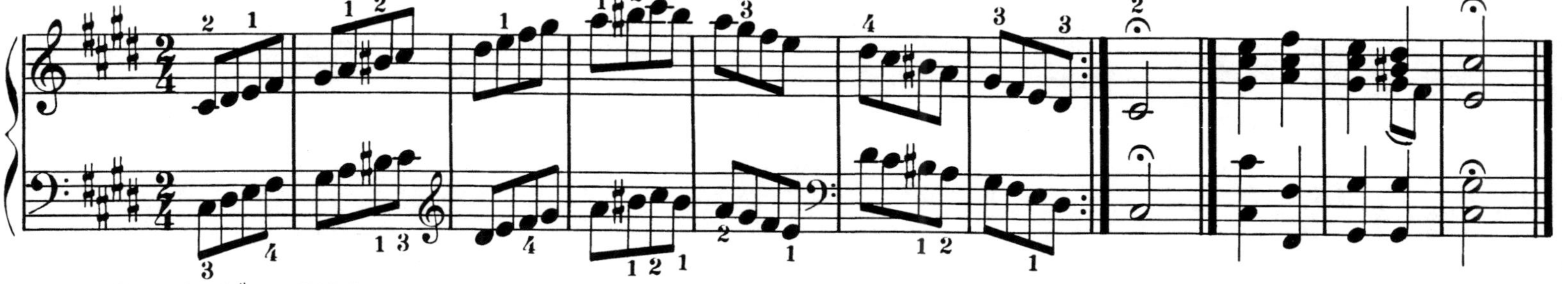

B MAJOR & G♯ MINOR

B major
identical with C flat major

G sharp minor (melodic)
identical with A flat minor

G sharp minor (harmonic)
identical with A flat minor

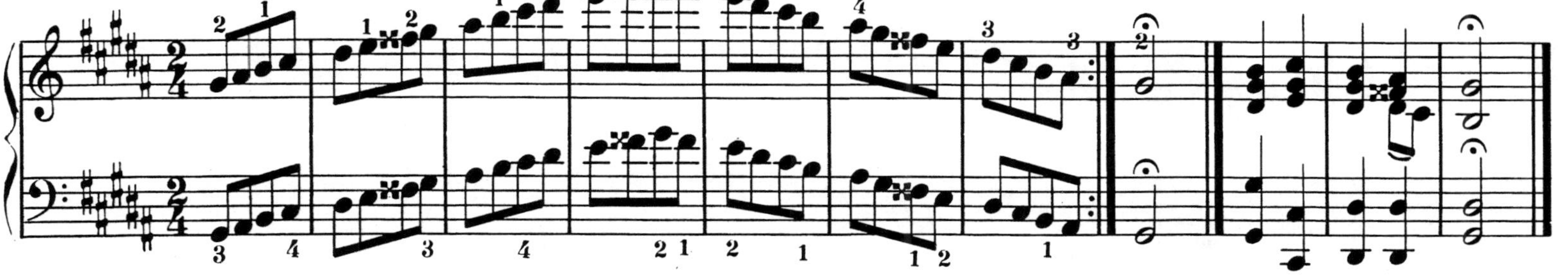

F♯ MAJOR & D♯ MINOR

F sharp major

identical with G flat major

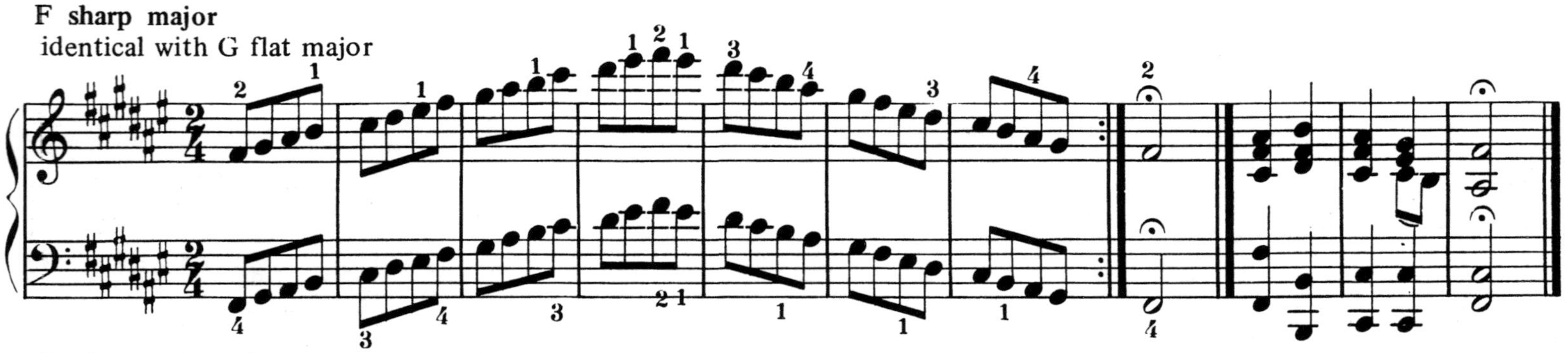

D sharp minor (melodic)

identical with E flat minor (which is more commonly used)

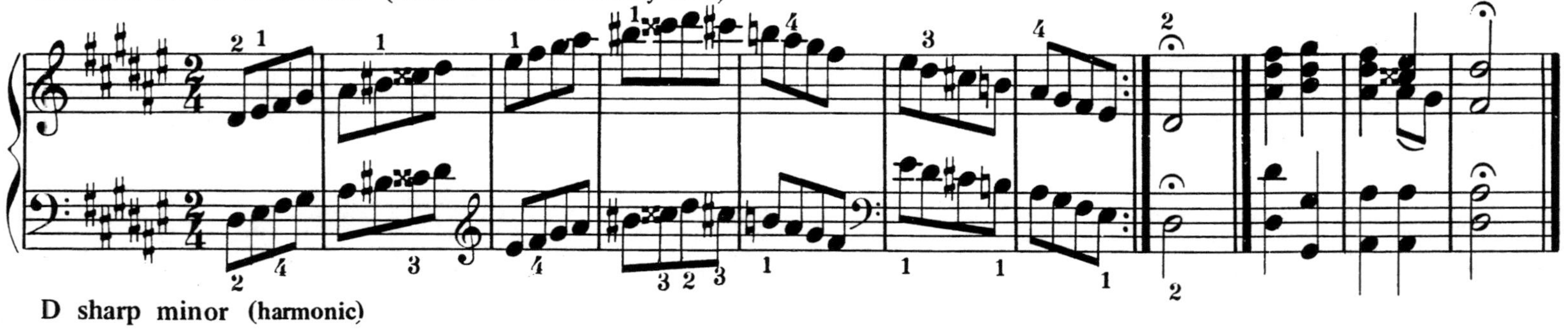

D sharp minor (harmonic)

identical with E flat minor (which is more commonly used)

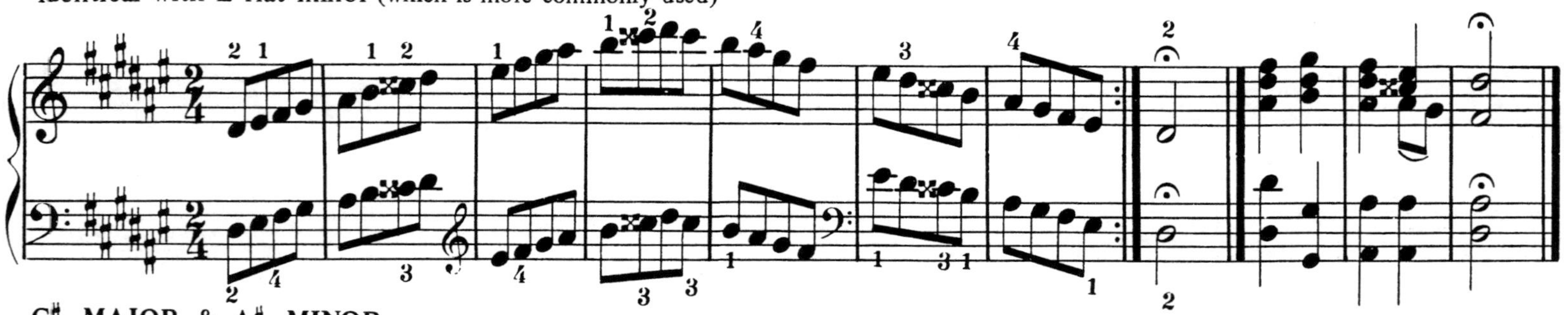

C♯ MAJOR & A♯ MINOR

C sharp major

identical with D flat major

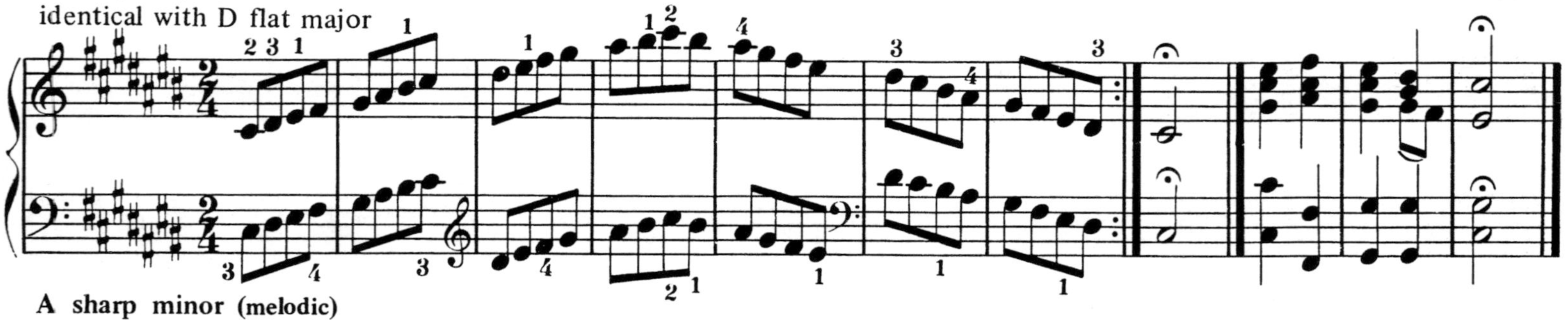

A sharp minor (melodic)

identical with B flat minor (which is more commonly used)

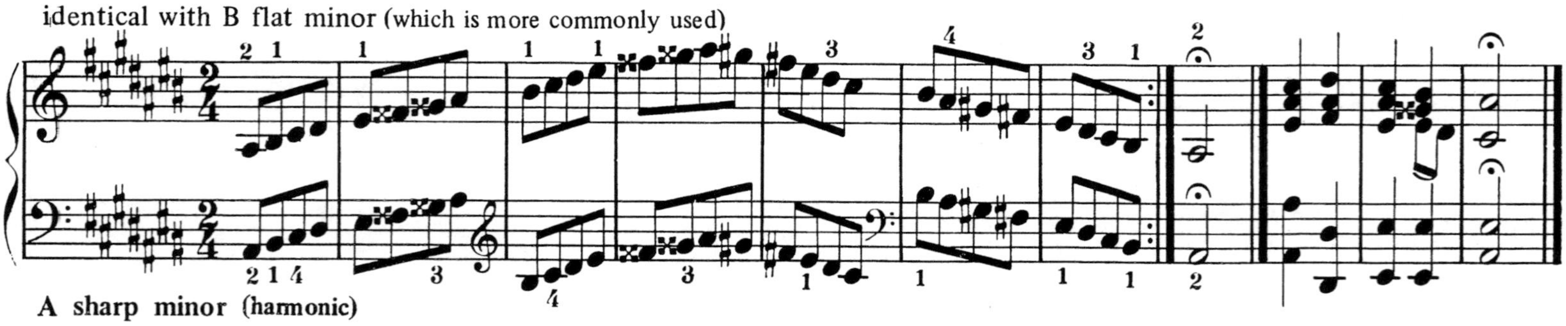

A sharp minor (harmonic)

identical with B flat minor (which is more commonly used)

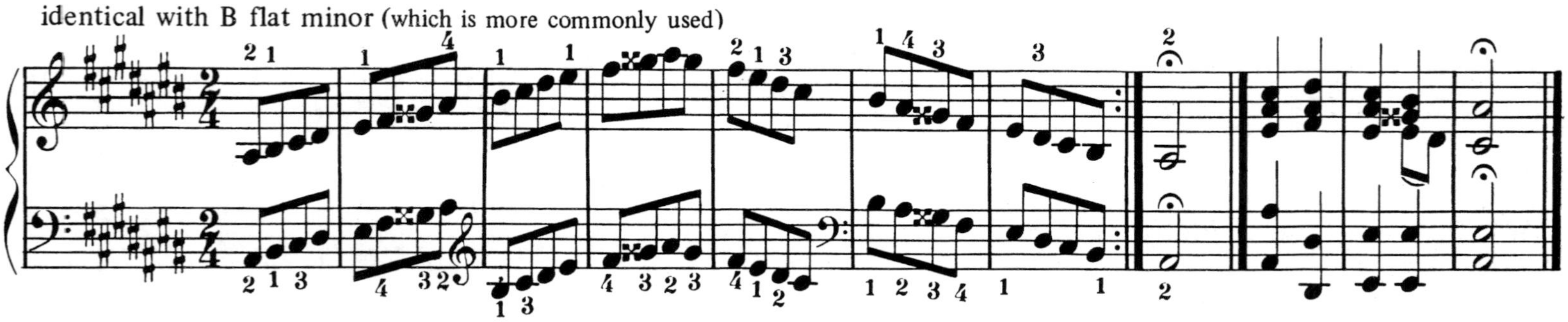

C♭ MAJOR & A♭ MINOR

C flat major

identical with B major

A flat minor (melodic)

identical with G sharp minor

A flat minor (harmonic)

identical with G sharp minor

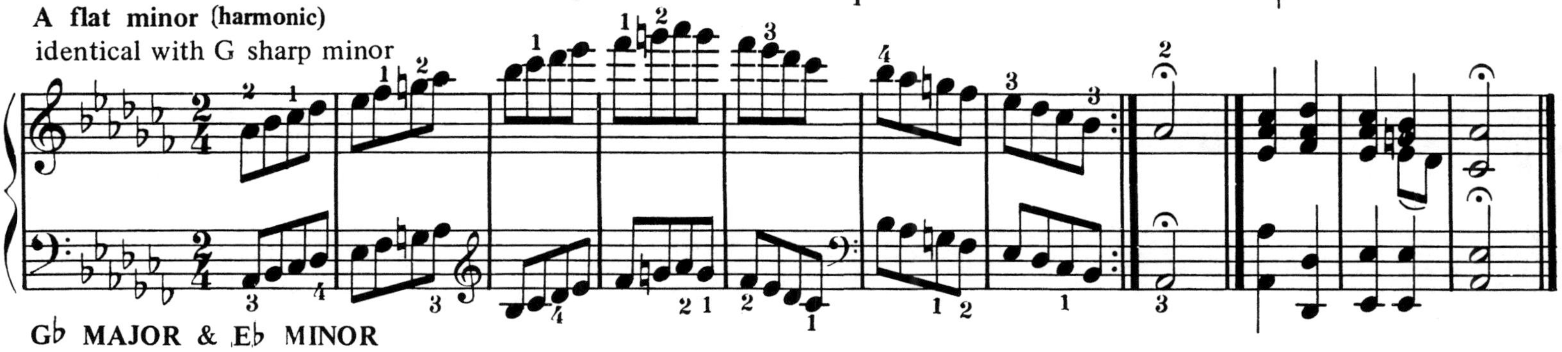

G♭ MAJOR & E♭ MINOR

G flat major

identical with F sharp major

E flat minor (melodic)

identical with D sharp minor

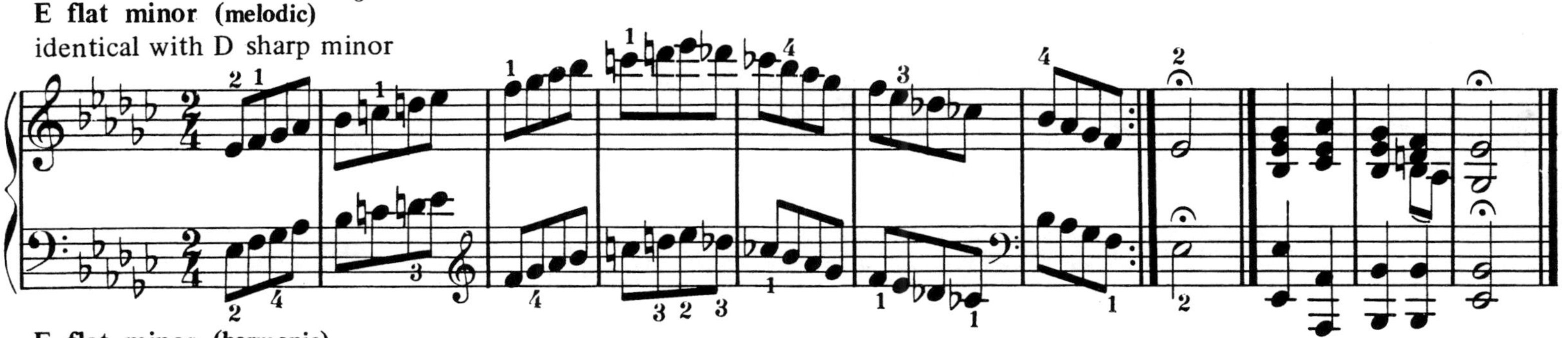

E flat minor (harmonic)

identical with D sharp minor

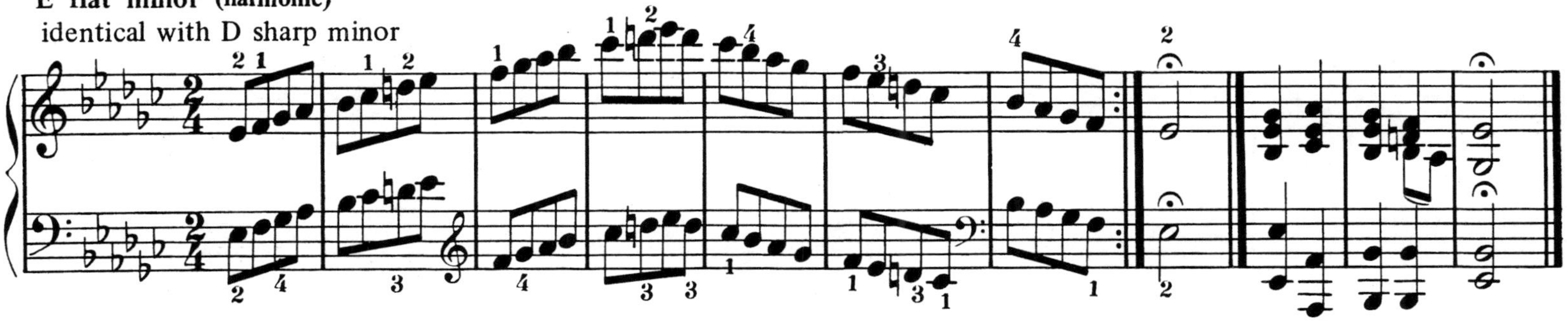

D♭ MAJOR & B♭ MINOR

D flat major

identical with C sharp major

B flat minor (melodic)

B flat minor (harmonic)

A♭ MAJOR & F MINOR

A flat major

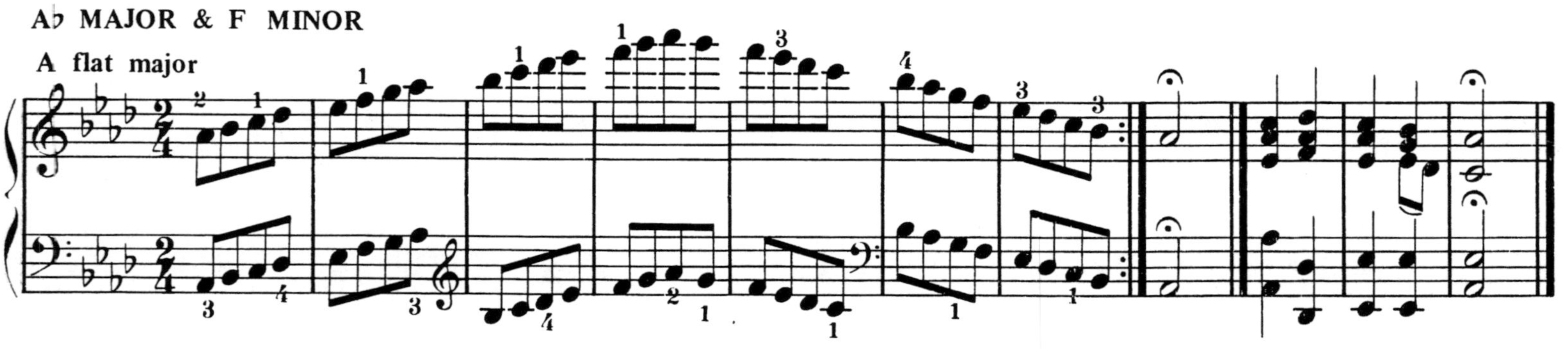

F minor (melodic)

F minor (harmonic)

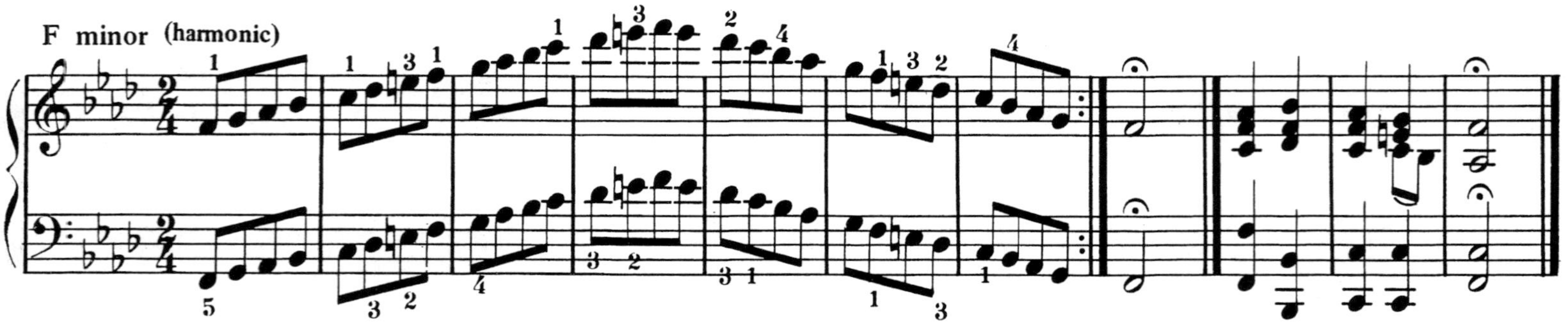

E♭ MAJOR & C MINOR

E flat major

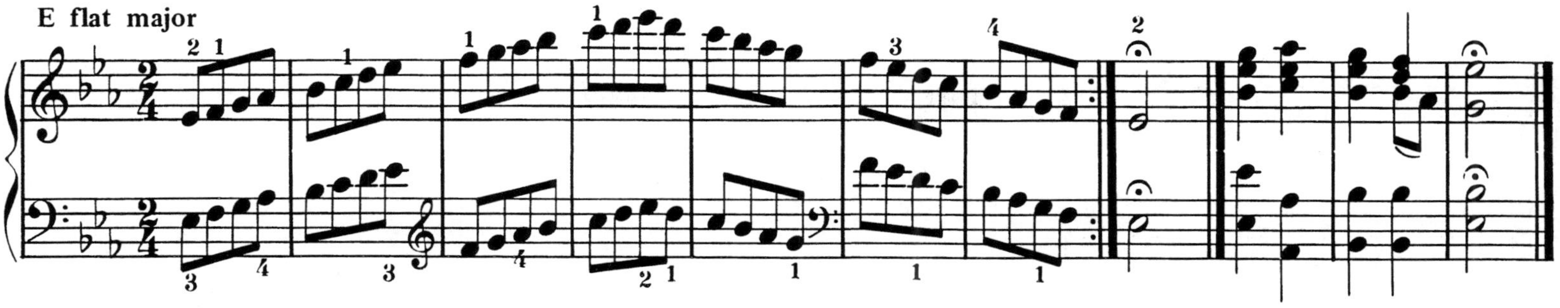

C minor (melodic)

C minor (harmonic)

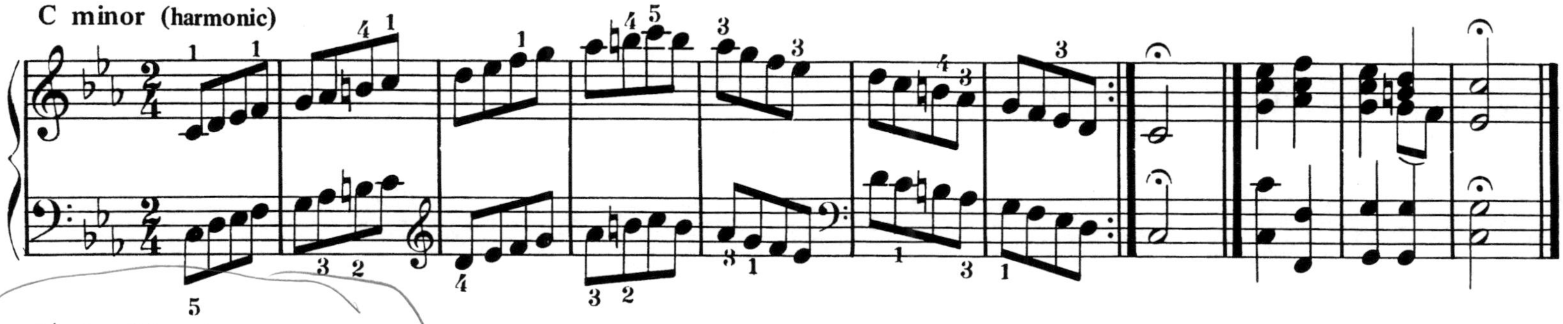

B♭ MAJOR & G MINOR

B flat major

G minor (melodic)

G minor (harmonic)

F MAJOR & D MINOR

F major

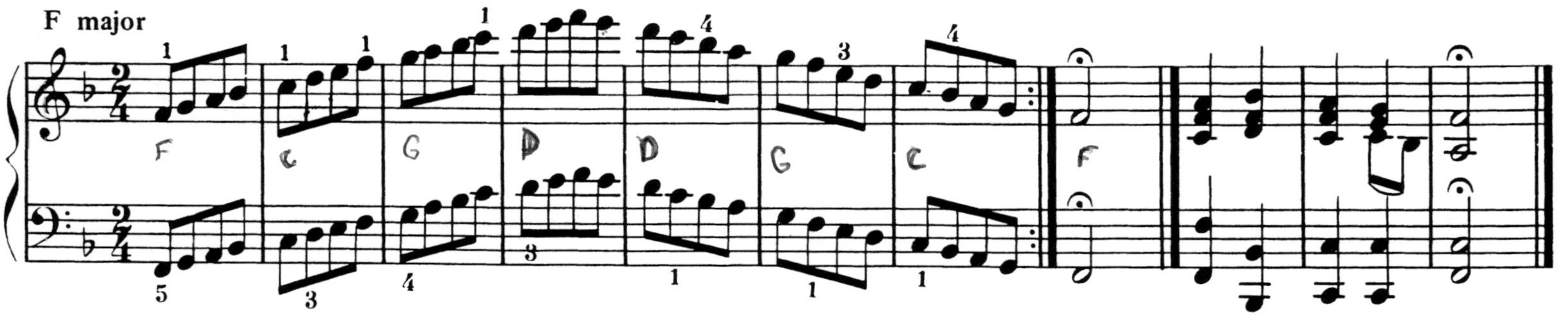

D minor (melodic)

D minor (harmonic)

THE CHROMATIC SCALE

Scales Combining The Major And The Minor

The major scale ascending, and the parallel melodic minor descending, used in some late 19th century compositions.

C major & minor

G major & minor

D major & minor

A major & minor

E major & minor

B major & minor

F sharp major & minor

C sharp major & minor

A flat major & minor

E flat major & minor

B flat major & minor

F major & minor

Scales In Varied Rhythms

Practicing scales in various rhythms will aid in developing facility and speed, as well as smooth turning under of the thumb. Here are a few suggested rhythms. Many others will suggest themselves to the student.

1.

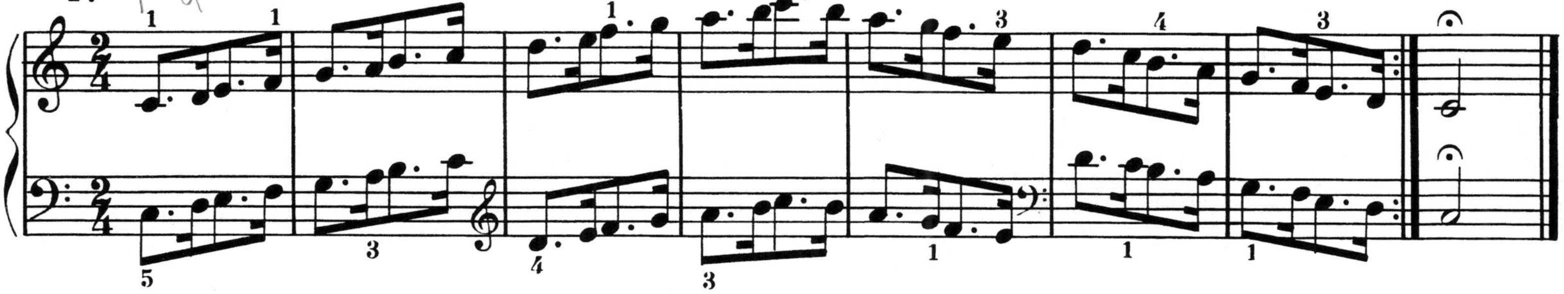

2.

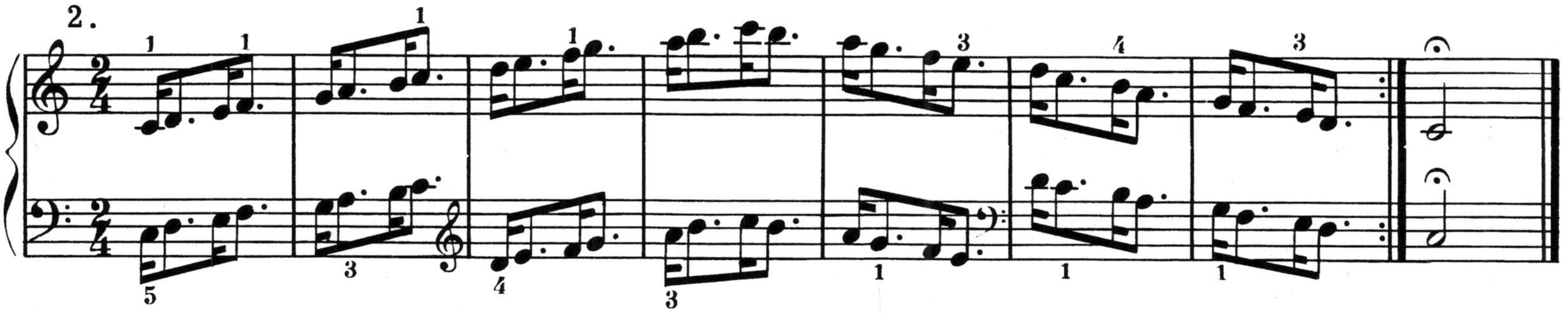

3.

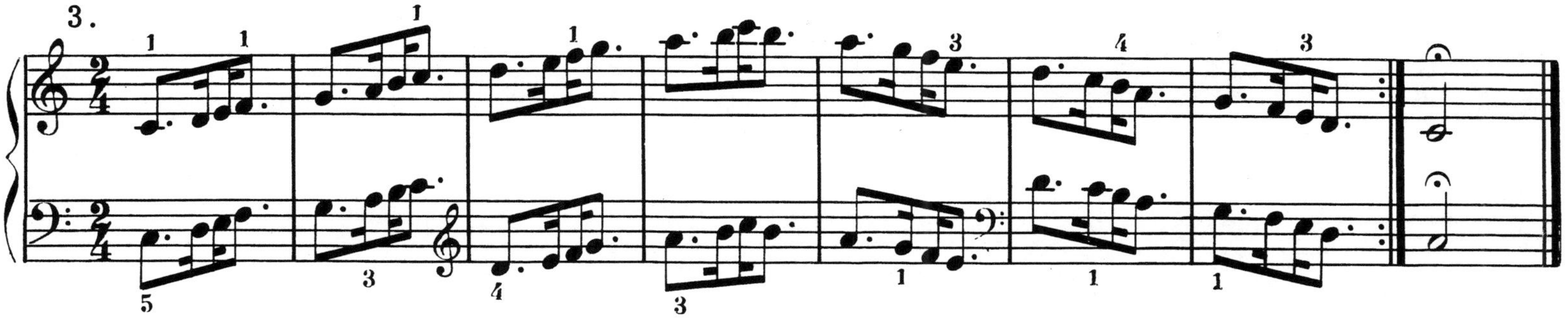

4.

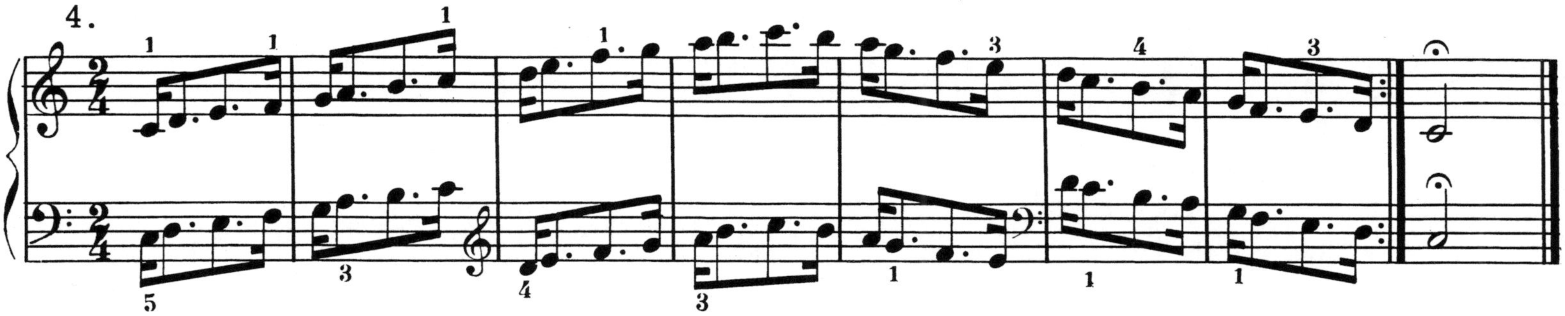

5.

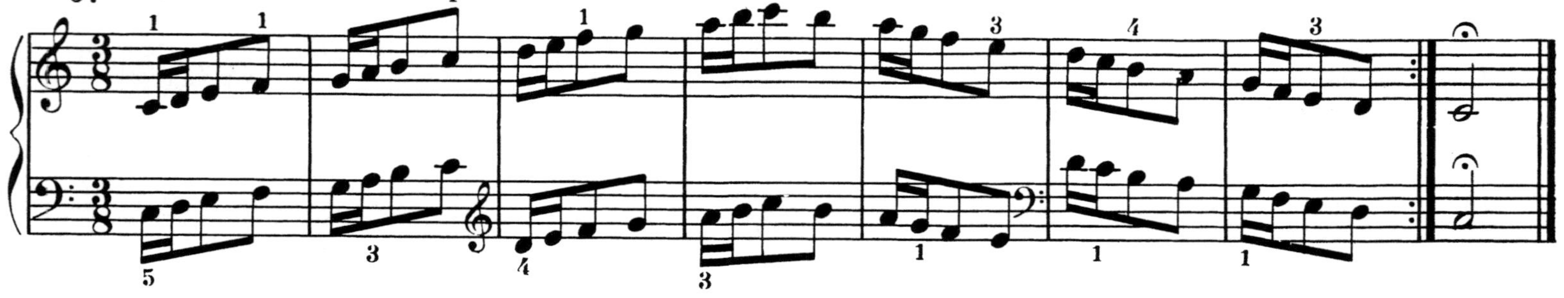

6.

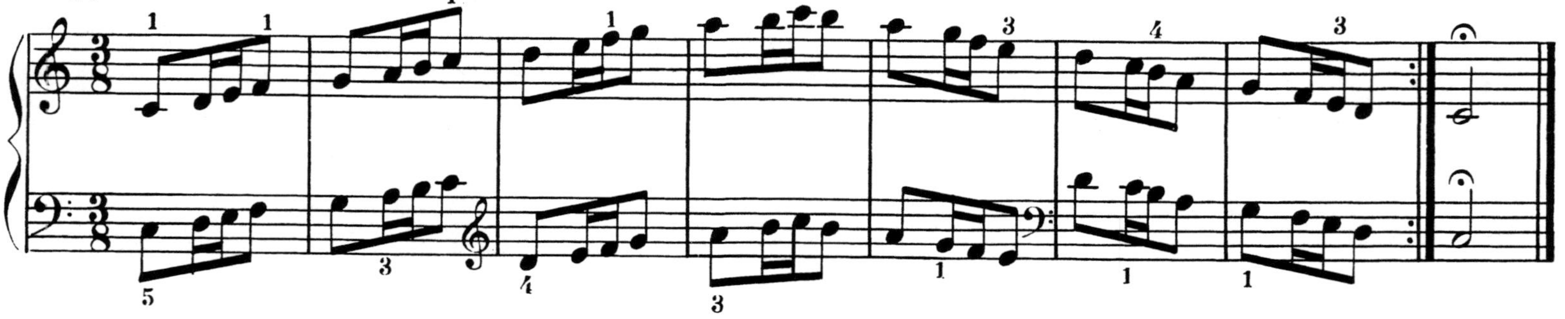

7.

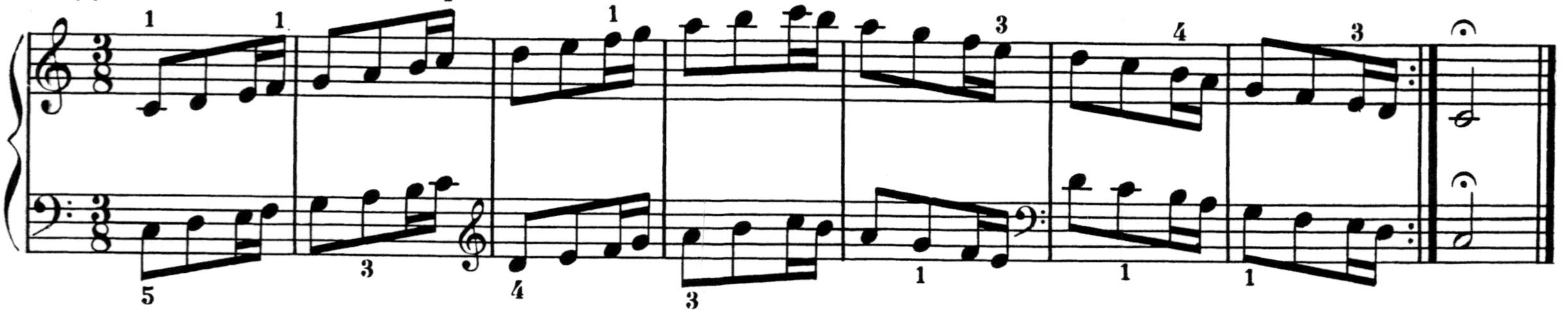

8.

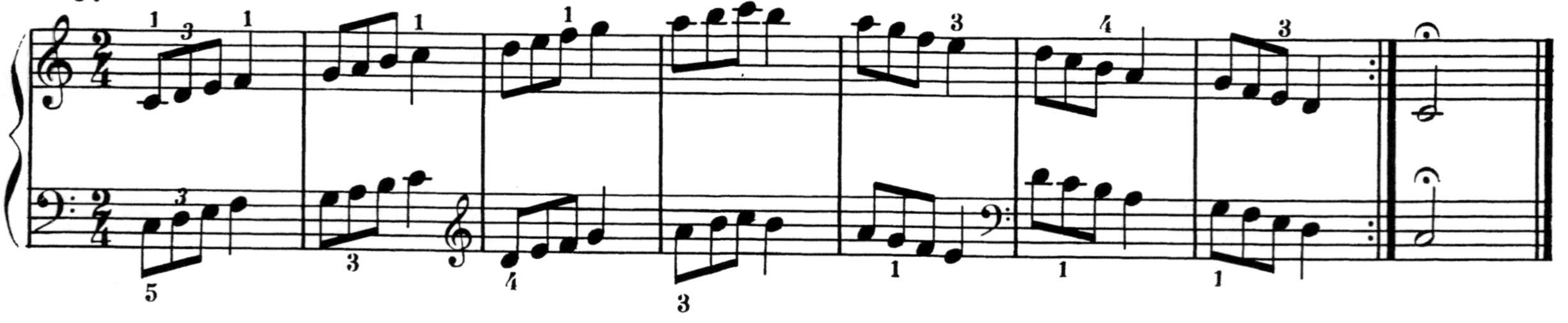

9.

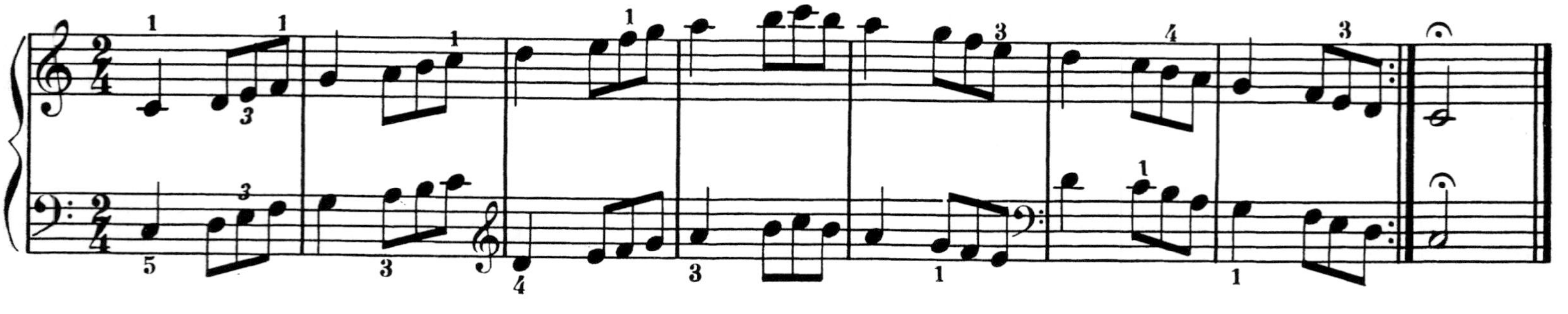